ARISE
THE
DAWN

POETRY AND PROSE
FOR NEW AWARENESS

VINCE DOWSE

VINCE DOWSE

ISBN-13: 978-1-9996429-0-7

arisethedawn@theworldiwant.org

www.theworldiwant.org

Available from Amazon and other book stores.

DEDICATION

To my wife Elizabeth.

To son and daughter Stephen and Philippa, and the memory of their mother Janet; to grandchildren Kahya, Felix, Dexter and Lola.

To all those who helped me right royally mess up my early life and hence forced me, out of sheer desperation, to look upwards and outwards for a better way. To all those who, in later years, helped me to find this much more fitting path.

"No Looking Back
The Way's Ahead"

CONTENTS

ACKNOWLEDGMENTS

Grateful thanks to my wife Elizabeth for her insights and patient understanding over many years and many circumstances, for her help in preparing the work, and for much detailed proof reading.

Thanks also to Elizabeth for the illustration accompanying the poem "Trees".

Thanks to Linn Law for the illustration accompanying the poem "I Am" and to Patricia Todd for her invaluable advice on format, publishing and marketing.

To the Centre Of New Directions whose philosophies have provided much of the inspiration for this work and whose members have given me so much support and encouragement over many years.

"The Soul Wakes Up
Revives, Renews"

PREFACE

This collection of poems is intended to help you to find your own way towards an enhanced awareness of yourself and the cosmos.

Such a step forward, with its implied shake up of established beliefs and perspectives can be unsettling. We can become disoriented and start to doubt our ability to keep our feet on the floor. I hope that illustrating something of what is to be expected will help smooth the way.

Some of the poems give suggestions about what may lie behind everyday reality. I put these suggestions forward as a framework of ideas for a new appreciation of yourself and your place in the world. They are not to be regarded as absolute truth or anywhere near complete. They are intended as a support in your own search for a meaning to life, for a vision of the future and to provide a basis for understanding mankind's purpose on earth and significance in the greater scheme of things.

It is important to draw ones own insights. Mine are expressed in the form of a commentary. This commentary is located at the back of the book for later reference if you wish, so as not to influence what you make of the poems before you have read them.

The poems can be read from a variety of perspectives. You are invited to allow time for any insights to emerge then come back for a second or more reading.

You may find that a phrase or verse keeps coming back to you. Keep it in mind. It may provide a meaning to a part of your life or an answer to a particular problem.

This is the pathway to new awareness.

Allow it through and nurture it.

Vince Dowse 2018

INTRODUCTION

What is needed more than anything else at this time is a sufficient understanding of our present state of being to encourage an integrated sense of who we are and where we fit into the scheme of things. Without such an understanding of the foundations for our existence (imperfect though it may be) we would be in a less than advantageous position to solve our current problems.

At our present stage of development as humans it is not easy to comprehend the full enormity of the cosmos or objectively describe our spiritual evolution through the sublime worlds that make it up. Poetry (and art) can provide a small and necessarily inadequate spy hole into those ineffable realms existing beyond our physical sight and the limited understanding of our intellect.

When we ask ourselves the question "what should I do?" or "who am I?" we usually look to our normal thinking processes, to the intellect and to outer sources of information and guidance such as the religions, philosophy or law and common practice. Often these can help enormously in a practical way as a means of determining our life patterns in conjunction with the world as it is and to develop the faculty of critical reasoning. After all we have to survive, we need to protect and nurture our families and to live in harmony with our neighbours.

These established approaches however, are very much determined by precedent and established ways of thinking.

Many people today, especially young people, feel that these established ways have failed. They turn to new media such as social networks and the internet to find solutions and to find hope.

But what if all of this outer guidance, both old and new is not working? What if "more of the same" is getting us nowhere?

There are many philosophical texts putting out almost as many varying views on the meaning and purpose of life as there are philosophers to write them. For this little book of poems there is only one overriding theme, the expansion of our own personal inner perception and understanding of the world we live in together with the patterns and principles that lie behind it.

Mankind has been through many stages of development. Each one broadly opening up more pathways of perception, more modes of experiencing.

We are beings of many faculties. We are progressing on a path of refining these faculties and opening new ones.

The forthcoming era for mankind is very much about the awakening of expanding awareness. We are entering a new and uncharted experience. We are transcending the familiar ways of understanding. They will no longer be our sole source of knowing and as a consequence the intellect may become disoriented and confused.

These new faculties are more akin to direct perception of truth than to intellectual understanding and reason.

It is said that all the information we need is within us and we only have to learn how to seek it out. Poetic license allows us to portray essences and to prompt the reader to delve within his or her own depths to retrieve an already existent knowledge. The insights are so gained without imposing a view or clouding the issues with detail that the intellect is not capable of appreciating.

In other words we appeal to the intuition - that unaffected truth seeking sense that allows our minds to appreciate something without reference to something else. It is the intuition that allows us to see beyond our habituated thought patterns and to break through the imposed and mostly erroneous views of what constitutes existence, what we are, where we have come from and, more importantly, where we are going.

Art and poetry by their appeal to our higher nature, can help us embrace this direct perception, direct knowing, direct understanding, without the necessity of logical explanation, intermediary authorities or reference to known accepted facts and concepts. Thus we become able to transcend distorted thinking, prejudice, and the limitations of the mind; in other words awaken the intuition.

This adventure of discovery will take us into hitherto unsuspected realms to become aware of the influences and patterns that lie behind the everyday world of the senses.

The process is very much akin to the time when we, as humankind, took on the power of thought and rose above the animals.

What if humankind is now again rising, this time above thought and into direct contact with these previously unseen worlds; entering a new dimension of experience you might say, clearing the pathways to a new dawn of perception?

And so to the poems...

"Play Your Part
In The Symphony
Divine"

THE JOURNEY OF MANKIND

Since ancient times in hallowed halls
The Word was ever told
That man is God and God is all
And heaven makes the mould

In Eden's day, man's paradise
The gods walked hand in hand
With lion, lamb, and unicorn
And husbanded the land

And then the Fall and man took mind
And heaven withdrew a distance
Mankind they say then forged his way
Without the gods' insistence

Then came a time of trial and tears
In accord with heavenly season
And cosmic masters graced mankind
With intellect and reason

Free will appeared and in its wake
Discovering cosmic laws
By learning from perceived effect
And making good the cause

Eons passed and minds grew strong
With nature as the guide
Through tribulation trial and test
Man couldn't be denied

The price it seems of such a gift
Was dimming of the means
Of seeing through to higher realms
To embrace celestial scenes

Thinking raised us from the mire
Of instinct, tooth and claw
Reason took us to the heights
Of science, logic and law

But minds have limits; thoughts are caged
The intellect is bound
To build on that already known
And that already found

The time has come to rise again
To meet man's next conception
To open up, see through once more
The doorways of perception

Once more the grace of heaven's embrace
And to see the Holy Light
No longer ruled by creed or rote
But served by clear true sight

Thus we go midst joys and woes
To landscapes yet unseen
Through heavenly paths of ebbs and flows
Towards the life serene

And so take heart and play your part
In the symphony divine
For soon you'll know without a doubt
Your place in the Grand Design

U235

Roses are red; chestnuts are brown
If you're looking for anthrax go to old Porton Down

Marigolds are orange; grasses are green
If you're keen on plutonium try Selafield sardine

The whole world's a rainbow under which mankind plays
With alpha and beta and hot gamma rays

Uranium fission is the source of our woes
The products send tingles to your fingers and toes

But as always we find within darkness there's light
The Thorium reactor will temper our plight

It burns up plutonium and hazardous waste
For the future of energy, it's in much better taste

We've unlimited feedstock and it doesn't melt down
So why don't we use it - make it the talk of the town!

But strong vested interests are active you see
Commercial, political and the military

So who will bring sense to this ungodly spree?
It's mankind en mass - that's you and that's me!

We don't want a planet cooked up in a stew
Exploited and ravaged for the sake of the few

Who through misinformation, secrecy and more
Beguile and betray us from board to shop floor

The answer, as ever is the mass frame of mind
From enlightened thinking of the bulk of mankind

The world's politicians cannot possibly resist
The will of the people that persists and persists

So open your minds, keep your reasoning straight
You **can** have an impact on matters of State

Don't be despondent when you see the display
Of a handful of people with what seems so much sway

They cannot continue to misguide and cow
If our aggregate wisdom will not so allow

So don't keep your silence, make known what you feel
Help bring in the future and fulfil the ideal

Of a world fit to live in, in safety and health
With freedom and justice and equable wealth

Your thoughts are important and help the rebirth
Of the collective awareness underpinning our earth

For holding the vision is surely the key
To establish the patterns of what life may be

So keep your eyes open and keep well in mind
That thoughts become actions when rightly aligned

And whatever your gender, seniority or youth
The way forward is openness, freedom and truth

WAS AND WILL

We're always in the present, the sages oft proclaim
What fits right now is all there is, the patterns play the game

The past is set, the future's yet
This moment is the better bet

For grasping one's essential itch
And finding that elusive niche

The rest is background froth and fret
Like weather and the National Debt

It isn't should or must or creed
That causes action to proceed

It's frame of mind that sows the seed
Arise! We're into freedom freed

From binding thought and hallowed rules
Imposed by obsolescent schools

There is no was there is no will
Just here and now and no until

To this the Sages do avow
That Heaven's here and Heaven's now

But though these wise men so avowed
We wind our way beneath a cloud

Of old beliefs and shuttered sight
As if a prison were e'er our plight

But there are no bars there are no blocks
The door to freedom has no locks

Save those illusions oft ingrained
That rule our lives as if enchained

By phantom powers that would have us kneel
But only if we think them real!

And hold! Today, the secret's out
There are no chains without a doubt

There is no overruling power
That can dictate, or make us cower

To imposed will or thought or deed
Without a ruse to which we cede

A visual trick or subtle words
That serve to keep our thinking blurred

From advertising's luring style
To political spin doctor's guile

The grip of these forces, now grown old
Is loosening and cannot hold

So what's **your** impulse? What's **your** seed
That's germinating, gathering speed

About to spring from fertile ground
A creative force that won't be bound

So seize the moment, here and now
Break through the limits and allow

Your talents, skills and vision through
And so reveal the real you

"The Door To
Freedom
Has No Locks"

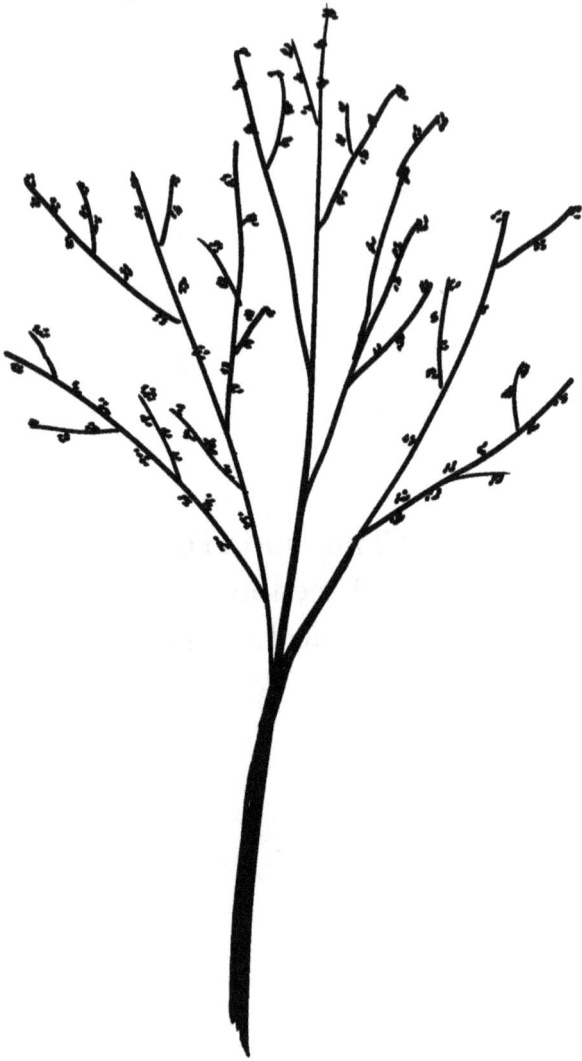

TREES

Have you looked in vain for a miracle?
Or a sign of the celestial king?
Have you looked at yourself in a mirror?
Or at a blossoming tree in the spring?

Do you hold there's no deeper reality?
Beyond the five senses or
Do you dream at times of the cosmos?
Do you wonder at times if there's more?

Think of beauty and friendship and courage
Of justice and goodness and grace
The intangible parts of our being
Part and parcel of the whole human race

But there are those who would have them diminished
Ridiculed even no less
Swamped by a materialist culture
The trappings of so-called success

But these gains are at best superficial
Though lauded by those who would rule
By creating a false sense of value
From the mundane, the gross or the cool

Our Establishment powers would have us
See just what they want us to see
For ignorance keeps us in bondage
But, the truth, sure, will yet set us free

But this wouldn't be good for business
Or maintaining the power of the few
To imprison the lives of the many
Cast down in a cold-hearted stew

We're held in the grip of illusion
That conceals the real and the true
By twisting our view of reality
With a spin-doctor's turn of the screw

Assailed by relentless distortions
From predatory press, net and screen
It's no wonder we're drowned in confusion
Our wits dimmed by powers unseen

Freedom is part of our birthright
Creative, with wisdom and worth
Without crushing control and coercion
Undermining the life of the earth

Would you like to be free of this bondage?
Unfettered by stifling lies
Then open your minds and your vision
See what's right in front of your eyes

For the miracles are right here amongst us
And freedom nigh under your wing
Have you looked at yourself in a mirror?
Or at a blossoming tree in the spring?

"Freedom Is
Part Of Our
Birthright"

LIGHT AND DARK

The Sun is coming out from behind the clouds.
It has been a long time coming.
The clouds were very thick and stormy.
They are dissipating into the nothingness
of the illusions they once were.

If we stand with our backs to the sun then
everything we see will be cast in our own shadow.
Too long, and too long is long enough.

The waterfalls fall; trees and plants grow.
Man and animals flourish regardless of the clouds.
Maybe the clouds are necessary
to hide the light for a while,
while we grow internally like seedlings,
that flourish in the dark and in the earth,
then need the light to develop upwards.

You are not alone.
All is as it should be.

"So Live
Within
Each Moment"

CO-CREATORS

Sitting in the office
Watching changing roles
Don't know what to aim for
There are so many goals

Take it forward slowly
Care for what is now
What's around the corner
Is charted anyhow

No need for angst or worry
Just enjoy the path you tread
Don't get caught up in the future
Live the here and now instead

Don't take on other's burdens
Just accept how they engage
Free choices are our birthright
Circumstances are our stage

Don't forget about your ego
Just learn where it has its place
It's the driving force for living
And is used to set the pace

Life is truly meant for living
Live as fully as you can
We are all divine quintessence
We are all part of the plan

Each one a co-creator
In the fabric of the world
Players in the cosmic light
Of the eternal plan unfurled

So live within each moment
As it passes on the run
For the future is not present yet
And the past is dead and done

Don't spend a lifetime guarding
Against events that may or might
You'll be wasting precious present
And be blinded to the light

It's your mind that shapes the future
And your thoughts determine fate
Too much fear of what might happen
Binds the power to co-create

This path is marked for everyone
And all things beneath the sun
For though we seem so separate
We are in truth all one

And our being is much larger
Than the bulk of us believe
In our own unique life patterns
Gods and egos interweave

This is how we were created
How we're meant to be on earth
So use its power wisely
With intent for higher worth

THE LAW OF THE SPIRIT

Now this is the law of the spirit
As old and as true as the Fates
And the soul that observes it will flourish
And the soul that ignores it stagnates

The route to salvation's not outside
Not given by dogma or rote
It is gained through the light of self-knowledge
By conscious awareness – take note!

From what does this consciousness free us?
From ourselves I would beg to suggest
From the collected dark stuff of the ages
Held deep in the frail human breast

There's no distant guru can save us
Nor ritual, colleagues or kin
For the ultimate path to our freedom
Is to reach for the Christ force within

This Christ force belongs to no section
No ruler, religion or race
It belongs to the whole of humanity
Each held in its loving embrace

And its presence is already active
The tools and the plan are in view
For the focus of change is within us
The means of progression is **you**

So however you see the Almighty
Whatever your race, creed or kin
Remember the law of the spirit
For the way and the word are within

"The Way And
The Word
Are Within"

THE SOCIAL ROACH
(THE UNITY OF NATURE)

Helmut von Scuttlebutt - a very fine roach
As cockroaches go - beyond any reproach
The thing, with his friends, he loved doing the most
Was to drop from the ceiling to snaffle your toast

His lady-friend, Snuffla – from pure Netherland stock
Is of noble descent through the line of Van Gogh
Her ancestral blood is the bluest of blue
And her family features in the Roach's Who's Who

Together they dine on the finest cuisines
From the pantries and kitchens of princes and queens
But their fondest delight is to frolic and feed
In the soup halls and sweatshops of Roachville-on-Tweed

Their mission in life is to further the cause
Of Roaches and others who help by the scores
To tidy the messes and clear up the waste
From spillage and garbage abandoned in haste

And to champion justice where e'er there's a need
Irrespective of lineage or kith, kin or breed
To offer good counsel, with decorum and grace
But where it is needed, to argue the case

Shy and retiring, oft misunderstood
Their ultimate aim is the general good
They work in the background but once in a while
Will make an appearance and put on the style

Hoping for friendship, acceptance, and Yes!
To requests for permission to clean up the mess
They are sociable creatures and like a good chat
So they'll sometimes approach you and may doff their hat

For meeting and greeting is a Roach's forte
And to make new acquaintance they'll go out of their way
Which is why when you're doing some everyday thing
They'll burst on the scene – at times on the wing

Creatures of company - loners they aren't
Each will come with his sister, his cousin and aunt
And try to entice you to join with the bunch
For dancing and prancing and sharing your lunch

So next time you see a Roach strutting his stuff
It could be Helmut or Snuffla so don't be too rough
He may be on duty - some spillage to tend
Or defending the honour of a six legged friend

Don't reach for the spray can or swatter or boot
Or otherwise zap without giving a hoot
Please do treat him kindly and allow him to pass
If you were the visitor he'd not be so crass

And know that you've spared a companion in life
A friend on the pathways through struggle and strife
For we all have our function, our value, our place
And we're all intertwined in the patterns of space

Each one a support to the other – and more
There's an interdependence – an integral core
We're one awesome system and we dare not encroach
On the delicate balance 'twixt mankind and Roach

"We All Have
Our Function
Our Value
Our Place"

THE DARKEST HOUR IS BEFORE THE DAWN
(THE HAND OF FRIENDSHIP)

In the rush of daily living
When you're flowing with the tide
You are caught up in existence
With no time to look inside

But in quiet times when all alone
And there's nothing more to do
The mask of daily living fades
And your self comes into view

When troubles mount and spirit's down
And it seems you've lost the plot
And the future seems intractable
Like the fabled Gordian Knot

Firm ground has gone your anchor's slipped
Life seems beyond control
Do not despair for what is there
Is the Dark Night Of The Soul

The Guardian Of The Threshold
Confronts us and we stare
As the truth is revealed before us
And our soul is for us laid bare

This is not a damning process
Though we feel it overwhelms
It's to pass within the fiery hoop
And on to higher realms

Though we feel alone and helpless
And we think we cannot stand
Support from those who love us
Is, as ever, close to hand

So reach out from in the darkness
Bid distress a fond farewell
When you take the hand of friendship
Shadows very soon dispel

LOVE - THE EVER PRESENT PRESENCE

Ere the dawn of time and space, ere the rise of suns and stars
Ere the first life raised its head upon the earth
Through the cosmos, very softly breathes a promise and a sigh
It's the force behind creation it's the guardian of birth
It is love o little seeker, it is love

When a man cares for a woman or a mother for her child
What attracts the two together, what binds them day and night?
When a bride and groom are married and are setting out in life
What's that just around the corner, what's there just out of sight?
It is love o little seeker, it is love

What fills the house at Christmas when the presents are all out?
When the frantic rush is over and there's silence in the room
What supports the strength of comradeship and the sacrifice of
war?
What drives the surge of springtime when the flowers begin to
bloom?
It is love o little seeker, it is love

What drives the course of planets as they cycle round the sun?
What keeps them in their orbits like solar kith and kin?
Or siblings round a parent or the bees around a hive?
Or the binding force of atoms or the mystic yang and yin?
It is love o little seeker, it is love

It's the universal healer; it's the ever present note
It's the light that ousts all bleakness and despair
It surrounds us with its presence; it's the essence of the world
It is conscious it is constant it is everywhere aware
It is love o little seeker, it is love

So when you feel you are abandoned and no one will understand
And hopelessness is flowing on the tide
Reach out to what surrounds you; take my hand that's waiting near
You'll find my hand is always by your side
Yes - this is love o little seeker, this is love

HOLD THE LIGHT AND STAY IN THE GAME

In the fields of human progress there are ups and there are downs
Like an ever moving balance in an ever moving round

In the eternal struggles of the forces high and low
It's mankind that holds the balance as the ancient peoples know

From the echelons of power down to grassroots, all the range
It's the action on all levels that brings about the change

Sharing joy in the successes, joint support when there's despair
Together we are strongest, and the key to this is share!

Let the presence in the action with the message be the aim
In all our interactions "Hold-The-Light And Stay-In-The-Game"

FUTURE IN THE PRESENT

As the oak is in the acorn
And the man within the boy
So the future's in the present
Live it fully and with joy

"The cosmic mirror from afar
Shows us who we truly are"

ARISE THE DAWN
(CLEARING THE PATHWAYS)

Clear the pathways dark and dower
That soul should shine with potent power

Clear the path for Spirit's truth
Of rust and dust from long disuse

Clear the way for right insight
No limits here - behold the Light!

Clear the source of old belief
Observe the turning of the leaf

Clear the stuck, outdated views
The Soul wakes up, revives, renews

Clear the road for forward tread
No looking back - the way's ahead

Clear the past of fixed ideas
Forge the way through new frontiers

Clear the mind of complex clutters
Simple sense lifts up the shutters

Clear the intellect's confusion
Intuition strips illusion

Clear the thoughts for true cognition
Mankind's next step **is** intuition

To reconnect with lost perception
Of subtle worlds and God's conception

Of human roles in the cosmic plan
From Golden Age to the Fall of Man

And to uncharted waters sail
As future mysteries unveil

The cosmic symphonies unfold
And we the players in awe behold

The glory as the spheres divine
To planets, suns and stars align

And as our destinies unwind
Enhanced perception, unconfined

Accompanies expanding mind
As gods and mortals intertwined

In cosmic unison advance
Mankind and angels join the dance

Eyes are opened, light revealed
And heaven's doorways are unsealed

Gone illusion, gone the veil
Truth no more beyond the pale

The cosmic mirror from afar
Shows us who we truly are

Enter insight firm and free
Awareness is our destiny

So as our earthbound spirits rise
Take up the challenge of the skies

The Soul at last restored, reborn
The night is past! **Arise the dawn!**

THE DOORWAY

There was a door, my own front door.

I walked through it
Out into the world.

It was freedom
Freedom from the stagnant life indoors.
Freedom from myself.

Indoors is the confined existence I have led in the past
Unknowingly leading my life
According to the whims and fancies of others.
Like a kind of conspiracy to stifle.

I walked on the beach
The transition between land and sea
Earth and spirit, Ego and Self.
Where we can truly be ourselves
At the moving edge of life.
Unfettered by the past and its restrictions
Unafraid of the future and what it might bring.

I walked out into myself and the universe
To dance with all there is.
Joy, rapture
A sense of living and breathing with the gods.
Unafraid of feeling I must conform.

The world will have me as I am
No more, no less.

There was a door
A door to my soul.
I walked through it.
And found.
I belong.

"So Where to Now?
What Path To
Take?"

THE THRESHOLD OF AWARENESS

When we look into the cosmos
With our telescopes and more
The immensity of space
Is coming closer to our door

When we delve into the atom
And the quantum world is shown
We are touching on the fringes
Of the seeable and known

Our scientific instruments
Let nature be revealed
And open up the vistas
That were hitherto concealed

These instruments are the organs
By which we get to know
And enable us to study
Where our senses cannot go

But the systems are constructed
To reveal earth's mundane face
And cannot take us onwards
Through the veils of time and space

So where to now? What path to take?
To open up conception
Of subtle worlds and higher planes
- The doorways of perception.

Our higher human organs
Are present here and now
Obscured by daily living
But ready when we learn how

To give a brand new picture
Of life's underlying core
(Not a modified understanding
Of what's been seen before)

Of what lies behind appearance
Of the everyday display
And the sense of higher levels
Which we think so far away

To find that they're much closer
Than most of us believe
Just a subtle change in focus
And we find we can perceive

Now the veils are being lifted
By the beings having sway
Over earth's true evolution
And mankind's advancing way

How will this awareness manifest?
How will we know it's true?
We have no clue or precedent
For these insights wholly new

What is colour to the sightless one?
Or music without hearing?
What's that whisper when we're quiet?
On the threshold of appearing

What's that thought just round the corner?
What's that view just out of sight?
It's the higher worlds approaching
- The dawning of the light

It is pure and clear perception
Not cause and consequence
It's the intuition calling
Our own truth seeking sense

We do not need a reference
Or guidebook writ to show
Its meaning, source or verity
The fact is - we'll just know

"Light Is Not Born
To Be Rendered Forlorn"

BE REBORN

You'll make a fine start
If you write from the heart
And the fire in your blood gives you room

For light is not born
To be rendered forlorn
Nor your feelings to languish in gloom

There's a passion it's said
Which when given its head
Will give you the edge over fate

When you take up the fight
Sun and stars light the night
And the bows and the arrows fly straight

So take up your sword
And slice through the chord
Of the old and the stuck and the worn

Gird up your horse
And give your full force
To your heart and your mind – Be Reborn!!

"Heal The
Underlying
Cause"

THE CLEARING OF THE LEVELS

Warts and blemish go away
Don't come back another day
Through the levels dark withdraws
Heal the underlying cause

Strengthen solar strengthen base
Through the systems shade displace
Quickly, quickly shine the light
Perfect patterns set aright

Body, mind and thought alike
Regain posture, perfect right
Imperfections not a trace
Perfect tissues meld in place

Past events that formed the cause
Are neutralised by cosmic laws
All systems now are free you'll see
The road is clear yourself to be

"Growing
And
Expanding"

I AM

I am the light in the body, drawn up by the crown.
I am weightless and non-material.
Like a chrysalis I am reborn.
I can dance. I can fly.
I am a butterfly fluttering and dancing in eternity.
I am a tree. I am solid.
I am rooted firmly in the earth.
Yet I can move gracefully like a ballet dancer
Flowing with the energy.
My wings follow the lines of force
like beautiful billows of lace.
I am an Empress – a Wise Woman.
My wisdom holds up my wings.
I am an Emperor
My energies drive the world.
I am faceless. I have no persona.
I am my soul.
I am one with everything through my faceless face.
I am a manifestation of God.
Like God I accept everything with love.
I am the oversoul of creation.
Spreading my wings
and animating all below with my spirit.
I am the spirit.
I am the shades of night and the coming dawn.
I guide and protect and animate.
I am love.
I have been born from the chrysalis many aeons ago.
Through countless lives I have travelled.
Growing and expanding.
I am the rocks; I am the flowers.
I am the animals; I am Man.
I am all.
I am everything.
I AM.

"I Am The
Weaver
And I Am
The Web"

EBB AND FLOW
(THE ETERNAL "I")

I am the flow and I am the ebb
I am the weaver and I am the web

I am the sower and I am the seed
I am the harvest and I am the weed

All is intentional, nothing by chance
Pen goes with paper and song goes with dance

Each event links to its time and its place
And interconnects with the patterns of space

Everything's spoken for under the sun
Each sparrow falling is part of the One

Earth - a reflection of heaven on high
Mankind - the connector, that's you and that's I

The whole of creation is held in the breast
Of the Source, the Creator, the Self, the thrice blessed

The unchanging one for whom we've no name
The choir and choirmaster, the eternal flame

But who are we meaning when we ask "who am I?"
If not the unseen, the ineffable eye

For wherever we look, whatever we see
It can never be "I", I'm sure you'll agree

Then who is this "I" who it seems can't be found
The being that hears but produces no sound

A child of the One of which we're a part
A unified consciousness here from the start

Of time and of space, of transcendence and Tao
The eternal presence, the here and the now

The original cause, the creator of dreams
Which I can observe, to make tangible schemes

The observer, the listener, the seer not the seen
As soon as we name it it's not what we mean

So seek not through the senses, you may go astray
For I am the life, the truth and the way

"I Am The Life
The Truth
And The Way"

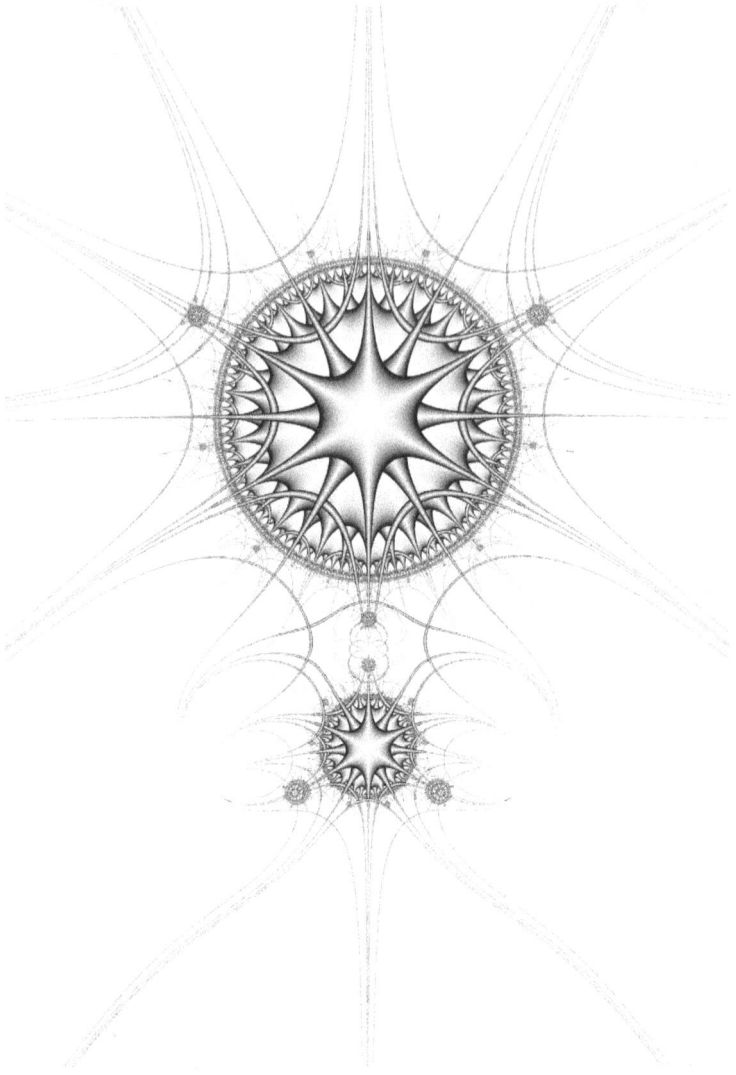

"You're
An Image
Of The Cosmos"

PATTERNS OF THE WORLD

When you link into the levels
Of the patterns of the world
You are touching on the power
Round which the cosmic builders whirled

Our thoughts are what defines us
And give structure to our drives
We live within the patterns
And the patterns form our lives

When your situation's daunting
And the world's in such a state
Remember you're connected
To the forces driving fate

You've explored all likely pathways
And you're still in disarray
Then seek out this connection
It will often show the way

It's your mind that draws these forces
And your passions activate
To link with the connection
Gives the power to co-create

Your intentions shape the outcome
Your focus forms the link
There's no need for strife or struggle
When you change the way you think

Get to know your inner landscape
Get to know it well
When you touch the light within you
Shadows very soon dispel

As the bee collects the honey
And the bees create their hives
So we're each uniquely fashioned
But together shape our lives

You're an image of the cosmos
With full power to co-create
In a partnership with Heaven
To build divine estate

The mutual might of self and soul
For fortune do conspire
So leave behind your doubts and fears
And follow heart's desire

SUBTLE POWERS

When you use the subtle powers
That the higher worlds bestow
You must subjugate your ego
To the gods and let it go

Remember you're a channel
Not the owner of the gift
And you've promised to give service
And to give the world a lift

Yes - remember you're a channel
For the energies to flow
Not the architect or planner
Or the one that makes it go

You're an instrument of heaven
In the service of the race
Get your impulse from the moment
Use the present as your base

Remember too that where you are
Is benefitting Man
So do not question why or what
It's all part of the Plan

This Plan may be a mystery
Well beyond our personal ken
But the cosmic mind is fashioned
From the single minds of men

We are each unique contributors
To the wheels within the frame
Of the cosmic choral symphony
Of the One that has no name

We do not see this conductor
And we often question why
But we are the choral symphony
The un-named is you and I

ON A LIGHTER NOTE

Somber minded people mostly expect us to approach religion in a similar vein rather than with lightheartedness and a joy for life. The motive for taking this somberness on board could be in order to appear as respectable and righteous members of society with only the best of thoughts and opinions, or possibly out of habit or even because of fear of a jealous God. None of these approaches indicates much understanding of the fundamental purpose of our lives. This purpose is not to demand conformity to any particular impressed belief or to show obeisance to anything, especially a demanding and unforgiving deity. It is to find our own development pathway on a journey of ever expanding awareness through higher and higher levels of consciousness.

One of the indicators of having a healthy perspective on life is appreciation of the humour in the sometimes intensely serious way we approach certain subjects. The poems in this section are an attempt to introduce a lighter side to how we view spiritual affairs.

"Together Attracted The Light"

THE SPIRIT OF HUMOUR

This aspiring old poet called Dowse
Believed he was brimming with nous
But his notions of karma
Of chakras and dharma
Were brought down to earth by his spouse

Though flustered, subdued and contrite
He thought things were really alright
For he and his wife
Were partners in life
And together attracted the light

"He Has Now
Understood
Both Evil
And Good"

OUT AND BACK AGAIN
(SEEKERS RETURN)

A fresh seeker from heaven was sent
And found himself on the descent
From Spirit to Matter,
He entered the latter
But didn't know what it all meant

His assignment before him was laid
And the Pathways to take were displayed
He had to refine
His spark of the divine
And the substance from which it was made

He plunged down to the mineral kind
Then a spiritual U-turn did find
Via animal and veg
Found himself on the edge
Of acquiring the quality of mind

He entered the first human race
And, un-briefed, at the helm took his place
On living starships
Which he used for his trips
Through the kingdoms of time and of space

On and on through the angelic worlds
By planets and stars truth unfurled
He saw from afar
Constellation and star
Where the cosmic creators once whirled

Via astral and mental and higher
Held by love and refined by the fire
To become more and more fine
And to cosmically shine
In the halls of the celestial choir

For aeons and eras and ages
He was guided by Devas and sages
To where seraphim fly
And cherubim sigh
And cosmic awareness engages

With gathering insight he saw
Infinity displayed in the raw
And that progress relies
On wide open eyes
And awareness of unbounded law

From naivety's innocent dharma
He'd progressed through the grand cosmic drama
He has now understood
Both evil and good
And the purpose of birth, death and karma

From the physical to the sublime
Jacob's ladder he aptly did climb
Now with no need to roam
He was finally home
And provided the theme for this rhyme

IMAGINE

Imagine if you will
An armadillo's quill
Or a feather from a jellyfish's back

Or antlers on a quail
Or a tail upon a snail
Or a polar bear camouflaged in black

There are whales in the sky
And pigs that have learned to fly
And turtles nesting happily in trees

There are butterflies that swim
And gorillas in the gym
Keeping fit so they can run away from bees

Have you ever seen a cat
With wings just like a bat
Alight at night on hairy horny crabs

And unicorns that cry
If a mouse gets in their eye
And buffalos driving chequered taxicabs

There's monkeys playing lutes
In pin-striped city suits
While elephants show their ballet dancing skill

And further into town
The nursing bears float down
With remedies for anyone that's ill

Meanwhile the singing rats
Parade in silk top hats
And bow to everyone who passes

Which would include a leprechaun
Or any horse called Sean
And all the spoilsport spiders wearing glasses

And then there's you and me
Observing from a tree
Dressed in woad and wearing winter wellies

Accompanied by cows
Suspended from the boughs
With pretty pictures painted on their bellies

There isn't any doubt
The above could come about
Do you really **think** I'd fib and fake it?

Impossible to conceive??
All it takes is to believe
The world in truth is only what we make it

THE SOOTHSAYER

A soothsayer claimed to be sure
He'd the key to unlock heaven's door
But his place in the plan
As the saints' middleman
Turned out to be just an allure

THE METAPHYSICIAN

A metaphysician took fright
While travelling much faster than light
He was late so they say
For a meeting next day
But arrived on the previous night

"If You Follow
The Light
Things Will All
End Up Right"

AN OLD FELLOW FROM KENT

There was an old fellow from Kent
Who harboured a spiritual bent
He was going for wings
But got caught up in things
Of a less than respected intent

This alarming old fellow from Kent
To the lower astral got sent
But his attitude mended
So from there he ascended
And to the higher echelons went

So if you find yourself on the descent
Have regard for this fellow from Kent
If you follow the Light
Things will all end up right
To a greater or lesser extent

"You Should Aim
To Have A Good Life"

ANOTHER OLD FELLOW FROM KENT

Another old fellow from Kent
Had a halo most terribly bent
To tell a sad story
He succumbed to self glory
And to the underworld went

He spent aeons exposed to the fire
Consumed by remorse and desire
But one day he relented
And soon he repented
And now sings in the celestial choir

Now this, as you may well remark
Is a fable for those in the dark
For heaven and hell
As we should all know well
Are both here and now - what a lark!

This means as you contemplate strife
You should aim to have a good life
If you ignore with impunity
The striving for unity
Then chaos and grief will be rife

"Common Sense Is
The Safeguard For Sure"

A MAN FROM NONSUCH

An aspiring young man from Nonsuch
Thought a Master had just been in touch
But the image as given
From the astral was driven
And wasn't in fact very much

Here's a caution for those who'd explore
As a spiritual conquistador
Take care of your life
For illusion is rife
Common sense is the safeguard for sure

Together with which we would say
That the curious are oft led astray
And what killed the cat
Could well lead to that
Which brings anguish and much disarray

For progress is not a mad race
All things have their time and their place
And these realms you're espying
Are not gained by prying
But by brotherhood, concord and grace

THE OLD LADY FROM STROUD

There was an old lady from Stroud
Who, of her standing with God was so proud
But her music was mired
When her harp she acquired
And she promptly fell off her cloud

THE YOUNG FELLOW CALLED PETE

There was a young fellow called Pete
Who was thought to be close to dead beat
But the light from within
Saw him through thick and thin
And he managed to land on his feet

THE YOUNG LADY FROM TRALEE

A young lady from West of Tralee
Thought her guru was such a grandee
When she asked him the way
He said "try the highway"
"Fifty guineas should cover my fee"

FOR BUDDING POETS

Like the tides within the ocean
Inspiration comes and goes
Just as the seasons cycle
So the spirit ebbs and flows

When your psychic system's static
And the Muses do not show
Just hold on to your frustration
It'll shortly not be so

For the Muses need a question
Or a theme to get them going
To ensure there's fertile soil
For the subtle seeds they're sowing

The muse
Come when they choose
Not at the yen
Of humorous men

71

The muse have a ruse
You think you choose
But the choice is theirs
Through one who dares

Mankind beware!
They're oft unfair
And send hot air
So - have a care!

For the mode of the ode's
To enlighten and goad
Not to light up the fire
Of an ego's desire

Though the muse confuse
They provide the clues
To future cues
And we can't refuse

There's no excuse
In the world's rich hues
When life construes
We have to choose

MISCELLANEOUS

Subtle conscious willing
When it's used aright
In the service of the Plan
Brings harmony and light

So leaders let the ego go
Abandon self for Soul
No need for struggle, stress or strife
In the moment find the goal

This is the future of mankind
For when all's said and done
Though seeming in so many parts
We are in fact all one

So use your talents wisely
For the spirit, mind and soul
And remember that the power of thought
Is what achieves the goal

Elizabeth D. of Brighton town
Was worried lest she let folks down
She had this special gift you see
Of seeing more than you and me

Not only had she clear insight
She had the nous to put things right
But woe is me! what do we find?
The general populace is blind

DON'T KNOW
(THE MID-LIFE CRISIS)

Don't know what, don't know where
Fate's a feisty, fey affair

Full of jibes and joys and woe
Pulls us to and pulls us fro

Lifts us up and drops us down
Makes us laugh and makes us frown

Then at last we see the light
Searching's o'er, the goal's in sight

Purpose calls, the path is clear
The ways unfold, the means appear

The past is done, the future's due
Life begins at forty two

COMMENTARIES

We start this commentary on the poems by considering the origins of mankind. Clearly if we could go back in time without limit we would be able to gain a picture of the origins of the universe itself and could trace developments from the beginning. However, the further back we go the more nebulous would be our understanding and perception of truth, and we would be more liable to error.

The ability of an ordinary living human being to discern such deep and mysterious truths is doubtful to say the least and we would be more in the realms of metaphysical speculation than true perception. In any case what would be the practical use of such an exercise in everyday life? So we start at the point where mankind evolved from the animal kingdom and first developed a mind with the glimmerings of self-awareness.

The Journey Of Mankind

"The Journey Of Mankind" suggests that we have a divine heritage and that at one time in our history we were directly in touch with higher intelligences who had the task of overseeing evolution; that we were led by them much as children are guided and protected by adults in a kindergarten; and that it was these beings who steered us through the transition from the animal kingdom to the human.

It was a relatively uncomplicated time, when we operated collectively. We were incapable of acting or evolving as fully independent individuals.

However, our consciousness gradually developed and we became self-determining. We were then allowed to go our own way, take our own decisions and learn from the consequences, so strengthening our abilities and discovering how to be individuals.

In parallel with this and as an integral part of our onward development, our ability to be directly aware of the guiding intelligences diminished and we had to learn to be self-sufficient by developing our own reasoning faculty.

Our acquired ability to think for ourselves raised us out of an instinctual, near animal-like existence and eventually allowed us to civilise into societies governed more by reason than brute force alone. In contrast to our ancient origins, we became able to act as self-conscious individuals.

In our present day we are at a transition point equally as significant as our transition from animals to humans. For the first time in the history of our cosmos we are regaining our ability to be in direct contact with higher worlds but this time fully self-aware and self-actuated.

This combination of freedom and direct contact implies a certain degree of empowerment together with the responsibility that goes with it. We see through the illusions from which mankind as a whole suffers. Life opens up before us in ways that we have hitherto not experienced. An unexpected mode of perception dawns and we see things from an expanded perspective. In other words we now take on board the enhanced consciousness towards which we have been travelling as part of our spiritual journey. Life takes on a new meaning and we see more clearly our role and purpose in the evolutionary process.

The forthcoming opening of awareness described in "The Journey Of Mankind" is not welcomed by all. Many people and institutions have a vested interest in keeping mankind in a kind of psychological straight-jacket. This desire for control has diverse origins, such as to preserve positions of power, possessiveness, maintain commercial interests, preserve outdated and limiting belief systems, vanity, personal ambition and many others.

It seems that these vested interests promote projects that could lead to very severe consequences for mankind as a whole. The accompanying publicity generally portrays them as beneficial and enjoyable or vital for our protection and survival in some way. Often the projects cause long-term problems in exchange for short-term profits.

One such is the proliferation of nuclear power and the consequential production of plutonium and other deadly radioactive substances. These products are so dangerous and long lived that they have to be contained for many thousands of years until they have decayed to a safe level. Protection from the radioactivity requires ultra-secure storage and the commitment of economic resources for many generations to come.

It often seems that nothing can be done to deter such projects, despite the good sense and sane thinking of many people.

However, there are subtle influences working through the mind of mankind. Before anything can manifest in the world it has to be preceded by thought. The more powerful the thought, the more likely it is to be effective. The misinformation, secrecy and other psychological trickery that tends to lead mankind astray, cannot match the collective will to the good of large numbers of people who focalise their views and agree on the right way forward.

Once it is generally known how the misleading influences are maintained then they lose their effectiveness. The factors in our society that would hold us back from creating a genuinely humanitarian world cannot survive in an atmosphere of openness and authenticity. As individuals we each have a part to play in this collective impulse.

The title of this poem, U235, is the scientific shorthand notation for the isotope of uranium providing one of the active components of most nuclear reactors.

Was And Will

From day one of our birth we are subject to many persuasive influences to believe in an imposed sense of who we are, conform to some assumed norm or code, to be this, that or the other. We are duped into accepting the authority of those who would impose their will on us and dictate how we should think.

There are two aspects concerning our life on earth that we need to take into account in our daily living. These dual aspects are personal fulfilment in its many forms and our role in the betterment of the world. Both of these are important and very much interrelated. Somewhat paradoxically, in following our true vocation and aspirations we are also fulfilling our part in the evolution of the world.

In the face of all the external pressures, we sometimes find it difficult to determine our true desires. Not only are we unduly influenced by experiences that we've had in the past, we are often held back by fear of an imagined future that in reality we cannot predict. We also have little direct control over the global environment or the circumstances in which we live.

Because of our conditioned belief systems we are often mistaken as to the true nature of these circumstances. It is as if we are imprisoned by clouded vision. However, the illusions and fictional beliefs are phantoms. The prison is a will-o-the-wisp that disappears as soon as we see through it.

When facing a challenging situation we should recognise that it is attitude of mind rather than anything else that determines outcomes. Of course action is always required in order to achieve an end but it is the patterns of thought that precede the action that are the primary cause. Although it often seems that we are shut in and limited by our circumstances, we are totally free to choose our own patterns of thought and so to influence future events.

As indicated in the previous poem, U235, we can grasp the moment and leave behind those influences that would try to impose control. We can realize our true selves and our own creative self-expression.

Trees

Most people at sometime or another wonder whether there is more to existence than we see with our five senses. Is there a deeper (or higher) reality underpinning our everyday world? The experiences we have in everyday life and in particular the information we get from the media, would generally have us believe that our physical existence is all there is or at least that there is nothing else worth bothering about. Often, because of familiarity, we don't appreciate what is right under our noses.

If what we see physically with our eyes is all that exists, where is meaning? Where did we come from? What is our purpose in life? What about our experience of the intangible factors, our qualities, our feelings, our thoughts and imaginations, those things which do not have an identifiable physical basis? From where does the wonderfully interconnected pageant of nature come from? Who or what within us does the experiencing?

In the overwhelming sea of impressions and information relentlessly beamed at us from all sides, the more perceptive and insightful side of our natures is almost drowned out of existence. Hence we are susceptible to having the wool pulled over our eyes by any self-serving interest who has control over the presentation of what we see and hear.

However, by taking a step back from a purely physical view of life; by opening our minds to what lies beyond, by becoming aware of what is going on, we neutralise the capacity of these self-serving interests to seduce us.

Light And Dark

For a long time now the human race with its many individuals has existed in a kind of semi-dreamlike state as if we were seeing reality through a fog of distorted beliefs and half truths. This fog has partly been maintained by external influences such as the media, lack of available facts, the apparent beliefs of others, our own reluctance to accept different views and so on. But also, our impression of the world is very much coloured by our own internal state, as if when we look into the fog we see a reflection of our own selves. Our view is filtered through our own specific screen of beliefs. Each individual's makeup is different, hence we all have a unique and partial impression of reality.

Nevertheless, the world is evolving in its chosen manner irrespective of our own individual impressions. Despite the limitations to perception, we are moving forward on an evolutionary journey. Eventually we reach a point in this journey where we feel the urge to reach upwards and outwards and to embrace a much wider view of the world than previously. Before we recognise this urge, we may well feel somewhat isolated and alone, and imagine that there is no support. We feel that we have gone astray. It is in this state of vulnerability that, given a willingness to embrace life, we discover that there has always been meaning and purpose to our existence, that the internal and external resources required to take us forward are available to us and that we are not alone.

Being in the "dark" is like a gestation period - growth that is to be encouraged but not hurried - a process that has its own time scale. Then, like seeds, when we are ready we experience an irresistible urge to reach upwards and outwards towards freedom and consciousness.

Emerging from the dark is not necessarily slow but is paced for protection, so that as the light increases so does our ability to see and navigate safely. Sometimes progress seems frustratingly slow, but in a moment, we find that we are the other side of a milestone in our lives. This milestone is often only appreciated when we look back at where we have come from.

Our lives are supported and guided from higher levels. Of course we still have to find our own way and take responsibility for our own actions. An individual's development is their own work, but though we may not directly perceive it, we are always in the presence of helping hands and our experiences always give the opportunity to evolve.

Co-creators

Although we might not be aware of it there is an overall plan for evolution. This plan is in the custody of intelligences belonging to the more subtle levels of our existence, or higher worlds as they are sometimes termed, wherein lie the influences and patterns underpinning the physical world. The forces of nature are a manifestation of these guiding influences.

Humanity in general and each individual has a part to play. In that sense we humans are co-creators of the future in a partnership with the higher worlds.

As we live our daily lives we may wonder what it's all about. We see ourselves taking on so many different roles and we may imagine so many different possibilities for the future. We can become confused and sometimes disheartened by the apparent complexity and multiplicity of choices. However we can take heart in the thought that we are part of a system. We are not alone or at the mercy of an apparently chaotic world.

We can very rarely predict overall outcomes. Over-attachment to the past or too much fear of the future often interferes with making the best choices. Our best course of action is to pay attention to our inner feelings, have a will to the good, and to deal with whatever presents itself to us in the moment. This approach can balk against traditional ways of thinking and on occasion may even seem to go counter to accepted good practice. Nonetheless, paying attention to our inner guidance, our intuition, puts us in touch with those patterns that lie behind the everyday world.

We cannot justifiably be held responsible for the action of others. We may of course have to modify our own behaviour as a consequence but, although we may act in concert, we each only have control over our own input to any given set of circumstances. In any case outcomes are the result of a combination of individual thoughts and actions within the framework of an overall pattern.

The Law Of The Spirit

We live within a framework of universal laws.

Like our everyday system of law and order, we are not prevented from transgressing the rules either deliberately or by mistake. However, we do have to face any consequences.

In the case of earthly "law and order", if we are found out then we are punished in some way or other under our man-made penal system. In the case of the universal law however, it is more that a transgression results in a disturbance that acts as an inner signpost. Then, if we are open to it, we find the way to reestablish our proper path.

Often our society's established sources of guidance, though useful at a certain stage of development, are sadly lacking when it comes to encouraging self-awareness and the insights arising therefrom.

We can find a certain amount of help from given information but in the end we have to look into ourselves to unearth the hidden factors holding us back and to find our way forward.

The Social Roach

We live in an amazing world. There is a tendency for the human race to be blind to its awesomeness and the intricate way it all fits together. In the intensity of daily living we do not find the time to simply stand and stare as the saying goes; we fail to admire the design of the overall scheme and the incredible attention to detail with which it has been conceived.

"The Social Roach", as it is written concerns cockroaches: a much maligned and not very well liked species, associated with unsavoury surroundings and a general lack of cleanliness. However, in this poem they are used as a somewhat dramatic symbol for nature and all its unfathomable ways and means.

In interfering with nature without full awareness of what is involved, mankind opens up the door to all sorts of undesirable side effects, some of which may have undreamed of and far reaching consequences. For example: the effect of insecticides on bees resulting in interference with fruit pollination, nuclear fission and the devastating results of unconfined radiation, soil depletion by over-fertilisation, and the long term consumption of processed food. In nature even the roaches have their purpose!

At our present stage of development it seems that collectively we have little desire to achieve more than a minimal understanding of the interrelatedness of nature and even less inclination to appreciate the more subtle processes underpinning the workings of our whole being.

So - humanity! Take care to fully evaluate all actions with wisdom and a will to the good.

When things are going smoothly and we do not have to face compelling issues, then often we do not come into conflict with our identity. We do not feel a need to question who or what we are; life is manageable, though possibly not as fulfilling as we would like.

When the mask slips or no longer satisfies its purpose then we may feel an urge to challenge its authenticity. Often this is accompanied by a feeling of being overwhelmed and out of control of our lives. This process can be extremely distressing. We are obliged to face up to our true characteristics and who we really are. It is sometimes called encountering the Guardian Of The Threshold or experiencing the Dark Night Of The Soul and is a milestone on our journey forward.

As ever, love is a powerful influence. Realising that we are not alone in our ordeal and accepting the support of those around us helps us to find our way.

Love - The Ever Present Presence

The influences we experience in our daily lives from acute conflict, hostilities between people, and the constant barrage of hypnotic suggestions beamed at us through traditional and the new social media, serve to blind our perception and conceal the reality of the love that surrounds us. In all this we could be forgiven for thinking that love is not a potent force or that in our time it has been overpowered in favour of antipathy.

The word love has many meanings ranging from emotional attraction and simple affection to such concepts as the original creative impulse or the binding force of the universe.

Love is possibly the most all-embracing human quality and is certainly the subject of more artistic and literary creations than any other topic. Yet it defies concrete definition and everyday rational description; it has to be sensed rather than expressed in words. Hence its meaning is perhaps best presented in a round about way to appeal directly to our feelings rather than the intellect. It is more a perception that can be known and hopefully understood when it is recognised. It nourishes the growth of our soul; it drives mankind's striving after universal brother and sisterhood, truth, beauty and goodness; it is an ever-present presence pervading the whole of existence. We only have to be receptive to experience it.

By suggesting just a few of the many things to look out for in life, it is hoped that this poem will help awaken the recognition of love, and support a more balanced view of the world.

We live in a world of conflicting influences; some of these work for us and support us in our evolutionary path as human beings; some work counter to this upward path and tend to drag us down. Nowhere is this more evident than in the fields of politics and conflict resolution.

Sometimes we seem to be moving forwards, sometimes not, but overall there is progress and it is always due to enlightened actions by people with a will to the good actively involved in the decision-making.

Behind the actions of the individuals directly involved, there is always a driving impulse that comes from those in support. This backing may be tangible or simply well wishing to create an encouraging environment and a certain sense of fellowship. The power of thought and intention to influence outcomes should not be underestimated.

The message of this poem is: for change to take place there needs to be focused action with a genuine will to the good together with positive engagement by people of like minds to create a supportive atmosphere bringing attention to the issues at all levels.

Future In The Present

This is a very short poem, but in its essence it contains a major clue to finding our way to a better world.

The whole of our future exists as potential in the present. It is the decisions taken in the present moment based on this potential that are the determining factors. The way to see it with unbiased eyes is to clear the filters, drop the imposed views, and be in direct contact with the fullness of here and now. A successful and humane future depends on having a sane and unprejudiced view of the world now.

An acorn requires nurture and nourishment to become a well-formed oak tree. A child needs the same from a human perspective in order to grow into a fully integrated and healthy adult. Similarly, the quality of tomorrow depends on our enlightened and caring management of today.

Arise The Dawn

"Arise The Dawn" is the linchpin and also the title of this collection. It hints at many of the ideas explored more deeply elsewhere and expands on the idea that we are part of a much larger reality than that which we see directly through our physical vision. It portrays from a spiritual perspective the current stage of humanity's development as multi-layered individualities, and where we fit into the structure of the cosmos. It suggests that we are at a singular point in our evolution as spiritual beings where we will possess fully developed self-consciousness. At the same time our perception will open to the higher aspects of ourselves and to the worlds beyond that which we can perceive with our five senses.

This opening of perception is the starting point for developing the insights into our true natures necessary to take our human race out of the current mess and towards a more enlightened evolutionary direction. We will see how, as human beings, we are travelling along a path of spiritual progression. This progression involves increasing recognition of, and participation in, ever higher aspects of the creative processes underpinning the development of consciousness. We are at a point where we are moving beyond the limitations of our intellect and baser emotions, towards the intuition and a greater awareness of the unity of our total being.

As portrayed in "The Journey Of Mankind" the more subtle worlds corresponding to our next stage of evolution are coming into view and we will be able to more purposefully cooperate with these levels. It is via the intuition that our perception will open up.

We each have an existing connecting pathway to finer levels. In the main these pathways have become very restricted by neglect and denial together with an unwillingness to rise above the allure of life based purely on the five senses. Information and insights have difficulty gaining passage and tend to be distorted by our old and stuck belief systems. It is as if a conduit has to be cleared by a metaphysical flue-brush to allow through the clear insight of the intuition.

This clearing is aided by reconsidering old ingrained ways of thinking, to be willing to seek and evaluate guidance, to be open to what arises in the moment and to have a conscious intention to welcome in a renewed state of being. With it we recover the lost contact with our guiding influences and the subtle domains to which they belong. We realise our roles in a greater plan for the world and see that we are in a previously unrecognised partnership for the advancement of its evolution. We are invited to consciously take our places where we truly belong, to join in the journey towards self-realisation and an ever-expanding appreciation of reality.

The Doorway

"The Doorway" reiterates a familiar theme - that of freeing ourselves from the limitations and restrictions of the past and opening up to a wider perspective.

Many of our ways of thinking and beliefs are ingrained into us during our early days as children and young adults. They originate for instance, from our family background, past figures of authority, our peer groups, the culture we are brought up in, the media in all its forms and so on.

The actual origins of our mental makeup are not so important, except to give a perspective from which we can work to free ourselves. What is more important is the awareness that we have internalised these influences. They have created a distorted view of our own selves and the world that has the appearance of truth.

As we go through life and gain our own experience, we often come to a point where these false impressions can no longer hold. We become uncomfortable with our identity and life. We may feel that there is no way out; we feel trapped by all the supposed restrictions.

Then we start to question! We may come to realise that previously held notions have no firm ground in reality; our true nature has not emerged or had a chance to be expressed. The conscious acceptance of this fact, and that it has come about through a series of false beliefs, brings with it a recognition that there is a way out. It is as if we finally see that there is after all a door to our self-realisation and that the door is not locked. In effect we make contact with higher parts of our being and become more at one with the universe as a whole

The Threshold Of Awareness

Scientific advances over the last few hundred years have been tremendous. We have explored outwards into the cosmos with our telescopes and other large-scale instruments. We have travelled to the moon and back and visited other heavenly bodies. We have explored inwards with our high-energy particle accelerators, into the microcosm of the atom and the strange world of quantum mechanics.

How far can we go in these directions? Where next? We may be approaching the practical limits of the current generation of instruments. Maybe it is time to introduce a new dimension to our understanding of physics. Perhaps further insights into the nature of our universe require an expanded view of what underlies the physical world and how to observe it.

Our present means of actual observation, though enhanced by technology, is strictly limited to the five senses.

Available information about our discoveries and insights is very much oriented towards visual modes of expression. It is our eyes that do most of our personal observation. However, the visual descriptions of the realities underlying the observations come from theoretical models, derived from measurements by instruments which do not provide direct perception; for example from detectors in particle collision experiments or data from space probes.

What if we could actually perceive the reality lying beyond the limits of our five everyday senses? What if we possess senses that are as yet inactive and we could develop these to give us direct perception of realities currently thought to be inaccessible or even non-existent?

It is suggested that such latent senses do in fact exist. As they emerge they will feel completely new to us. We are coming into a time when we will learn how to wake them up and use them to further guide our research and exploration at the frontiers of our knowledge.

Be Reborn

"Be Reborn" applies to everyone, but is particularly concerned with those of us who strive to write or express what we see, feel, or perhaps aspire to. Our inspirations are not meant to be kept to ourselves, but expressed for the stimulation and enlightenment of all. When we are creative there is a buildup of potential and a call to action from higher levels of our being.

If we are willing to provide an outlet for this call then the consequent relief of pressure encourages further flow of new material. We are lifted out of stagnation and beyond the everyday; we feel a fresh impetus to life and a revitalised purpose to existence.

It is as if we can be reborn simply by following our own creative visions and impulses.

Clearing Of The Levels

This poem is a kind of invocation, an expression in symbolic form of a wish for alleviation of the trials and tribulations of life, a wish for a kind of elixir to cure all ills. However, it points out that there is no "magic" solution to our problems. Our current state of being is always in some way the result of how our lives have developed in the past, our history taken as a whole.

The solutions to the difficulties and enigmas of life are found by firstly identifying the binding causes (shine the light on them, make them fully conscious); then having brought them to light, to release them by taking responsibility for leading a conscientious and ethical life according to common sense and a will to the good. We are then freed from these old constraints and can follow our true destinies.

To find the strength and courage for the work to bring about the release from old impediments, we need to look after our health and boost the energy required to maintain our sense of purpose.

I Am

We have no difficulty in thinking of a lump of apparently amorphous solid as being one identifiable named object and simultaneously understanding that it consists of specific atoms. Similarly we can envisage the ocean as a unified mass of individual globules in the form of raindrops condensed from water evaporated from this same ocean.

Is there a parallel with ourselves? How would it be if we could see ourselves as individual beings, each differentiated from one single state of unified consciousness and on a journey of return to this state once more?

Is this issue simply one of perception? Perhaps we are approaching the point where we could grasp such a concept and might we see the validity of it?

"I Am" is one of several poems which raise the question of who we are behind the facade of appearance. It reflects the idea that we each originate from the one consciousness, and having grown through the experience of many roles and many situations, we return "home". We experience ourselves as being the one sum total of each and every one of our experiences.

This poem follows in a similar vein to "I Am" in suggesting that we all share in a world of unity where all things are in a synchronicity, each with its purpose within a coordinated whole. It again brings up the question of "who am I?" and "where do I fit into the vastness of the cosmos?".

The suggestion is made that "I" am a point of consciousness, a differentiated copy of the whole of existence that has followed its own unique path, yet has never severed its identity with this whole. To our everyday way of thinking this is a paradox - the part being unique, with its own set of characteristics and qualities yet also containing within it all the other parts.

We could ask ourselves "who or what is making the journey through existence?", "who or what is collecting the experiences?" or "is it the point of consciousness which identifies with the whole and just the experiences which make up the uniqueness?". We could also ask "if I am this point of consciousness why can't I see myself?". These questions cannot be answered by reference to the intellect, which is limited in its reasoning capability by sets of rules and predispositions. It is these rules that create the paradoxes. Reality is reality and we get to know it through perception not through concepts and reasoning.

We have to rise above the perceptive level of the intellect. At our present state of development this means the opening of the intuition. As already put forward, the intuition is our truth seeking sense, our way of appreciating something without reference to any predetermined impressions or ideas.

As awareness expands we become able to appreciate the reality of ever finer levels of existence.

We suggest in the poem that "I", differentiated, yet coincident with its all-inclusive source, cannot be seen because it is always facing outwards; it is the observer not the observed. What we see, and may believe to be ourselves is merely our mechanisms, our characteristics, our accoutrements. For the same reason we cannot see our source, our creator because we are coincident with its being and are therefore always facing outwards.

There is a word in the English language that we cannot apply to anything which is outside ourselves; yet we can all use it simultaneously to refer to our inner selves.

This word is "I".

We are not alone. In addition to the everyday world and the people in it we are part of a wider structure that creates patterns within which we have our being. We are not normally aware that this system even exists yet it has a profound effect on the way we conduct our lives. In turn, our individual thoughts and feelings have an impact on these patterns. It is as if existence unfolds as a combination of our own and higher influences.

We once again touch on the theme of the opening of perception beyond the everyday world of the five senses.

We sometimes get to points in our lives when it seems that whatever we try with our familiar approaches we cannot find a way forwards through our problems. We are stuck. We are missing something and it is not to be found using the usual methods. What if we need to change our approach, revise old ways of thinking and look beyond?

Perhaps somewhat paradoxically, looking beyond is equivalent to exploring our own depths, or to put it another way, "to find the light within". Focused intention can provide the necessary inner link and direction.

In conducting this exploration we may well encounter a sense of the unity that underlies our being; a unity which overcomes the doubts and fears that we may experience when embarking on our true aspirations in life. We realise our connection to higher guiding intelligences; we appreciate the beauty and fulfilment of mutual cooperation in creative endeavour.

Subtle Powers

This very much compliments the poems "The Patterns Of The World" and "Ebb And Flow" It reiterates the theme that our progress in the world depends on cooperation between ourselves as human beings and higher guiding intelligences.

It is humbling to truly appreciate our position as human beings in the vastness of existence. This appreciation implies a certain degree of awareness of higher states and an intuitive grasp of the significance of causes and effects beyond those belonging to the physical world.

Relegation of personal desires to the back burner is required together with an acceptance that our role in life is not primarily personal advancement but to be dedicated to the service of humanity and the development of the world. In addition we have to recognise our relative insignificance in the overall scheme of things, and that even with somewhat advanced awareness, we each possess only a very limited vision of the whole truth of existence. We have to relinquish our egos in favour of higher ideals and in so doing we recognise that we are integral parts making up a unity of being far beyond the restrictions of everyday life.

The Spirit Of Humour

Humour: that abstract quality whose definition has defied the efforts of philosophers and intellectuals down the ages. However, defined or not, we naturally recognise it and benefit from it when it is experienced.

It lends colour to a world that would otherwise be seen more in shades of grey. It lightens our moods and puts forward a more joyful context in which to view dreary or even somber matters. It calls attention to the foolish and preposterous, and helps us to see through our own limitations while preserving self-respect and dignity.

It can point out, transcend, and clarify one-sided thinking in a socially acceptable way, allowing alternative perspectives to bypass our prejudices and so introduce concepts that would in other circumstances be rejected. It cuts through self-importance and pomposity. Cultural inhibitions can be overcome, allowing us to reveal (to ourselves) previously suppressed perceptions and aspirations. It can shift our perspectives without relying on somewhat dry logic and reasoning.

In the journey of self-discovery, which can be thought of as an alternative expression for expansion of consciousness, we are presented with challenges to a plethora of previously held convictions and coveted notions about ourselves and others. Humour smoothes the way for alternative, sometimes disquieting, new ways of looking at things. It can reveal mistaken thinking and illusory beliefs.

As the new age thinker said to the devil.
"This is not hell and I'm not in the least bit warm"

Out And Back Again

"Out And Back Again" presents the same theme as the first poem in this collection "Journey Of Mankind". In a more humorous limerick style, a symbolic description is given of the journey from our origins as differentiated points of consciousness, undertaken in order to learn self-awareness and to evolve by passage through all the levels of reality. In effect this is a journey inwards (or downwards) to materiality, followed by a return, enriched by the experiences gained on the way.

Our exploration takes us through all the kingdoms of nature and begins with a descent into physical matter. We then ascend through the plant and animal kingdoms to a transition point where our minds awaken; we achieve individual self-consciousness and we become human.

Our diverse means of travel on this journey consist essentially of organic and various subtle vehicles or bodies. These have been developed and refined on the way and are poetically termed "living starships".

From the human stage we progress through more subtle kingdoms under guidance of higher beings. We gain an appreciation of our cosmic origins and the meaning of our journey of expanding awareness. We also gain an insight into the framework of cosmic law that underpins the growth and stability of the universe. We get to understand the processes and purpose of the mechanisms of creation.

Finally we are "home" with our accumulated experience ready for a new creative cycle to begin.

Imagine

The fringe of imagination's lunacy.

Believe in yourself and self-determination!

Immediately understood by your children without explanation.

We Are Reaching
"Beyond
The Prophets"

UNVEILING THE FUTURE

We have to accept a certain limit to what we can perceive and what we can understand. This limitation is due to the fact that we live in the physical world as human beings at a certain level of development. Our main modes of perception are our five material senses – sight, hearing, smell, taste and touch. These senses are supported by the various enhancements available from science and technology.

Traditionally our main mode of understanding has been through the intellect. Many of mankind's major advances, especially over the last few centuries, have been via the intellect. We have seen scientific advances in, say, the last 200 years or so which have possibly overshadowed those achieved in the previous 2000.

What if the intellect itself is now due to be augmented?

There's been much publicised just lately about the raising of consciousness. Such accounts need to be coherent and intelligible, and related to life as it is experienced at the everyday level.

So, what is it? Can it be understood at all?

Humankind seems to have a vested interest in making things complex. Perhaps there is an underlying belief that nothing can be worth having unless it is difficult to obtain and even more difficult to understand. However, the underlying principles are simple.

Consciousness is rising. We have seen our understanding of the natural world increase in leaps and bounds, and there seems no slowing up of this progress. We are probing into the microscopic world in tangible ways and with our theoretical speculations. Quantum theory and its application is revealing a structure to the world that would have seemed pure fantasy only a few years ago. We are able to describe physical life in ever more detail as the structure of DNA and the human genome are unfolding.

We are probing into the macroscopic world with our telescopes and space laboratories. A world full of the wonders of the Cosmos is rapidly unfolding as we peer ever further into the night skies and towards the birth of the physical universe.

The vastness of the cosmology of the universe and the infinitesimal physics of the quantum levels are together drawing us towards an understanding of the very large in terms of the very small. We will be able to understand the macrocosm and the microcosm as the unified reality that they really are.

What is this, we may ask, but one aspect of the raising of consciousness?

We are seeing in-depth questioning of our established religious beliefs and practices. The barriers between the major religions are slowly dissolving and we are becoming more aware of the common fundamental ideas. The distortions that have been created by those wishing to impose their own power are coming to light and we are gradually approaching a more enlightened view.

Transparency is emerging in politics, government, the military, banking, and other domains. In many ways this is forced, and is resisted by the institutions. The resistance is a stabilising influence, but also tends to slow down progress and cause much of the disruption and instability we experience as change takes place.

A degree of discomfort occurs. We find that life can become difficult especially for those directly involved in spearheading new approaches. In all the turmoil, it sometimes seems that we are being drawn backwards. There are still wars, poverty, injustice, corruption and many more things that need attention.

There is much to do. Nevertheless the veils of ignorance and limitation are being cleared. Social development is mostly in the direction of evolution.

What is this but another aspect of the raising of consciousness?

Our moral awareness is becoming more enlightened. We do not now send children to clean chimneys; we are aware of, and do not allow, the social conditions under which the bulk of our population lived during the industrial revolution. The artificial barriers between nations are coming down and there are a growing number of people around the world who are beginning to appreciate the wider human family.

We recognise the need for universal health care. Complimentary therapies, light, colour, sound and the influence of subtle energies are gradually being accepted in our healing professions.

Overall, our institutions are reforming into units that are more suited to the currently evolving world.

Many of the world's major, and minor religions have predicted that there will be a shift in human awareness and a shakeup of our ways of living and relationships around the present time. We have the Mayan prophecies, Revelations, The Apocalypse. Each of these, in one shape or form, involve an opening of awareness. With this comes a major reappraisal of our understanding of life, and the relationship of human beings to the Cosmos.

We are at a time in history where there is an unprecedented unveiling and distribution of knowledge over the whole of society.

Like the ocean tides we have to ride with the flow. Our role, as human beings, is to cooperate in this movement and to manage the consequences at the level of everyday life.

And there's more. Not only are the frontiers of knowledge being rapidly opened. The frontiers of awareness itself are similarly becoming available for exploration.

What does this mean? It means that new faculties of appreciation and awareness are becoming available to mankind as a whole. In past eras these faculties have been available to the few who had advanced sufficiently to be able to act as the forerunners, establishing the ground on which others would tread.

The larger part of humanity will soon be able to appreciate, as if for the first time, the realities currently lying just beyond our threshold of awareness; beyond the veil, as it is sometimes expressed. The veil is becoming more transparent and we will see our true place in the universe. We will share consciousness with the worlds and beings that underpin and provide the essential qualities of the physical world of the five senses. In a manner of speaking, we will walk hand in hand with the gods.

You may well ask - if this is so, why does it seem to take such a long period of time? Why can it not just happen?

We must consider that the world is a challenging place and we are becoming more sensitive. If our eyes were immediately fully opened, most of us would have great difficulty living in the world while simultaneously possessing the sensitivity for appreciation of higher aspects of life.

We could be overwhelmed. Mental and emotional stability could be put at risk. We therefore have to develop a social system that provides the necessary support for these times.

Why should this be so? History has shown that new aspects of human knowledge and experience have met traditionally with opposition, sometimes of an extremely virulent nature. This is in part due to the suspicion that naturally appears in established thought when confronted with a new opening in understanding.

We are now coming into an era where the faculty of direct perception is becoming available. This faculty transcends thought, transcends traditional ways of looking at things, and very often flies in the face of established authority. It lies beyond logical argument and reason by precedent. In other words, where knowledge becomes directly perceived, it is liable to bring a weakening of authority in its wake. We become custodians of our own lives.

So! What is this awareness? What are we looking for? Can it be described?

The answer can only be expressed circumspectly. Words do not exist in our current vocabulary for a completely new reality. It has to be experienced. We are entering on the threshold of the unknown. (Not just the already known clothed in a new appearance). The nearest we can get, as has already been said, is a sense of knowing; a perception in full clarity; an awareness within ourselves that is beyond question.

We may well have great difficulty in putting the new insights over to others. Art, literature and poetry can at least allude to these truths and can provide support and encouragement as new areas of experience unfold.

However, the difficulties of communication do not matter that much. The perceptions are very rarely intended for communication to others. The revelations are individual. Their validity is internal, and it is in the internal appreciation that we find their usefulness.

We may allude to what we have seen; but an inner perception, by its very definition cannot be seen or appreciated by someone else. The underlying truths can only be perceived individually. They are not for public airing. In any case, such an airing, if attempted is more likely to attract hostility than anything else. We believe in ourselves and hold our own council.

An exception is when like-minded individuals get together for the specific purpose of sharing their experiences. The individual jewels in the crown shine together to make the crown complete. Similarly, each individual light when shared, produces a more composite image, a balance of things seen from many different viewpoints.

Each one of us acts like a filter on the truth. We have our own particular ways of looking at things. In our humanness we have our blind spots. The cooperative sharing of views and perceptions can help us to arrive at a balanced appreciation.

The future of spiritual learning is no longer so much to be through an individual teacher or guru who knows, while the pupils are ignorant. It is much more to be through the individual revelations and insights shared within a cooperative group.

We are going into an era in which mankind's learning will be self-generated and "Beyond The Prophets".

You only have to look at the diversity of human life and the myriad opinions and viewpoints held to appreciate that no one person or group has a monopoly on the truth.

We are leaving an era where the mass of humanity has been influenced largely by collective unconscious impulses. Witness the destructive mass manipulation of whole populations such as the spread of Nazism in the run up to the Second World War and subsequently in the rise and fall of many oppressive regimes and one-sided extreme politics.

There are of course varying degrees of these collective forces. There have always been some free thinkers with individual perception who could stretch beyond the collective thought patterns. This faculty of perception is gradually emerging in humanity as a whole. We are being freed from the restrictions and limitations.

This is not necessarily a comfortable process. We have to face the collective fears of mankind, and we invent belief systems in order to protect ourselves from the uncertainty. We seek to reinforce those beliefs if we feel that they are threatened.

It is the accompanying fears that are behind most of the unhappiness and conflict in the world. We see the repercussions demonstrated in material possessiveness, racial discrimination, religious persecution, draconian laws and so forth.

However, the veils of unawareness are lifting. We will soon be directly aware of the meaning and purpose of physical life as part of a much larger and wonderful universe. Like seedlings, we have grown in the darkness of fertile soil and are making our way into the air and into the light to blossom into the next phase of our development. We are about to be released from the fears of our unknowing. We will be more aware of the structure of the universe and the security of our place in it. No more will we be subject to the feeling of being hopelessly lost in a bleak and lifeless universe. The meaning of existence will become clear and undeniable. There will be no more feeling of isolation and estrangement. Certain knowledge of the unity of all life will take its place. Loneliness and fear of abandonment or death will no longer have any substance.

Death itself will take on a new meaning. No longer will it be seen as something to dread, an end to consciousness, an extinguishment of life. It will be seen for what it really is, like birth, a transition from one state of being to another. Not to be feared but seen as a celebration of a fulfilled life; a return to those subtle worlds from which we originate; a return to the home from which we have temporarily travelled to experience the adventure of life, one life among a succession of lives.

Then there is freedom, freedom from the limitations of restricted thought and fixed points of view, a general lifting of the veils and a release from the self-imposed views of who we are. With the opening of perception it will no longer be possible for us to be manipulated by those who would have power over us. We can take up the freedom that is our fundamental true state.

The secrecy and misinformation that are the means whereby people are subjected to control, subservience and exploitation will no longer be possible. We will find that our institutions will gradually move towards a state of openness and allowing, mostly because, as awareness expands, there will be no place to hide the truth. The means of control and manipulation will simply slip away into the illusions that they once were and we will be free to follow our unique paths of creative fulfilment.

"Openness
Freedom
Truth
And Inclusivity"

A CLOSING MESSAGE

When looking for the usefulness and true validity of a situation :-

Avoid those that have the characteristics of Control, Secrecy, Misinformation and Exclusivity.

Be prudently open to those that have the characteristics of Openness, Freedom, Truth and Inclusivity.

For these are the hallmarks of our future.

Clarity of vision
Is the mark of coming days
Release from limitation
And extension of our gaze
To transcend the present boundaries
And open up the door
To universal knowledge
And the freedom to explore

Insight and perception
Will expand the field of view
And life will only sanction
What is genuine and true
Openness and freedom
Are the keys that show the way
So onwards, upwards, wakening
And let consciousness hold sway

— — — — —

This Is The End
Of The Book
But…

It Could Be Your
Next Step Or Even
The Beginning…

Of Your Exploration
Into The Realms
Of Higher Consciousness.

May The Wind
Be Always
With You…

May The Sun
And Stars Be Your
Compass...

And May Your
Own Self Be Your
Guide And Mentor.

ABOUT THE AUTHOR

Vince Dowse first hailed out of Kent
On a scientist's life he was bent
He studied up North
Then ventured forth
And to chemical processing went

Chartered scientist by occupation
His days filled with dry computation
He thought there was more
So he knocked on the door
Of the cosmos to find his salvation

He wanted to share his impression
Of the insights now in his possession
He searched round and round
For a means to expound
And found poems his mode of expression

After several years of vexation
He set down his thoughts as narration
And so he was drawn
To write "Arise The Dawn"
To help people seek inspiration

Now that he's semi-retired
He finds himself highly inspired
To spend much of his time
In metaphysical rhyme
Writing insights just freshly acquired

www.ingramcontent.com/pod-product-compliance
Lightning Source LLC
Chambersburg PA
CBHW060940040426
42445CB00011B/942